PAKISTAN INSTITUTE OF DEVELOPMENT ECONOMICS

Building Genuine Islamic Financial Institutions

Asad Zaman

PIDE WORKING PAPERS
No. 111

September 2014

PIDE Working Papers
No. 111

Building Genuine Islamic Financial Institutions

Asad Zaman
Pakistan Institute of Development Economics, Islamabad

**PAKISTAN INSTITUTE OF DEVELOPMENT ECONOMICS
ISLAMABAD
2014**

Editorial Committee
    Dr Abdul Qayyum   *Head*
    Dr Durr-e-Nayab   *Member*
    Dr Anwar Hussain   *Secretary*

All rights reserved. No part of this publication may be reproduced, stored in a retrieval system or transmitted in any form or by any means—electronic, mechanical, photocopying, recording or otherwise—without prior permission of the Publications Division, Pakistan Institute of Development Economics, P. O. Box 1091, Islamabad 44000.

☐ **Pakistan Institute of Development Economics, 2☐14.**

Pakistan Institute of Development Economics
Islamabad, Pakistan

E-mail: publications@pide.org.pk
Website: http://www.pide.org.pk
Fax: +92-51-9248065

Designed, composed, and finished at the Publications Division, PIDE.

CONTENTS

		Page
	Abstract	v
1.	**Introduction: Contrasting Spirits**	1
	1.1. The Great Transformation in the West	1
	1.2. The Functions of Banks	1
	1.3. A Paradox of Islamisation	2
2.	**Contrasting Views Regarding Human Behaviour**	3
	2.1. Economic Models of Human Behaviour	4
	2.2. Islamic Concepts About Human Behaviour	5
3.	**Generosity and Waqf**	6
	3.1. Historical Role of Waqf in Islamic Societies	7
	3.2. Necessity for Revival of Waqf	8
	3.3. A Subtle but Radical Difference in Goals	8
4.	**Trust and Dar-Ul-Amanah**	10
	4.1. Betrayal of Trust: Money and Banking	10
	4.2. Islamic Alternatives: Safekeeping of Real Assets	11
	4.3. Circulation of Wealth	12
	4.4. Three Way Split	12
5.	**Qarḍe-Hasna: The Key to Social Capital**	13
6.	**Accumulation of Wealth**	14
	6.1. General Principles for Accumulation of Wealth	15
	6.2. General Purpose Institutions	16
	6.3. Special Purpose Savings Institutions	17
7.	**Concluding Remarks**	18
	References	19

ABSTRACT

Since the spirit of Islam is in stark and violent conflict with the spirit of Capitalism, the form taken by institutions designed to express this spirit must also be different. Capitalist financial institutions are designed to support the process of accumulation of wealth, which is at the heart of capitalist societies. Central to Islam is the spirit of service, and spending on others, which is expressed by diverse, service-oriented institutions, radically different from those dominant in capitalist societies.

JEL Classification: E15, G2

Keywords: Financial Institutions, Islamic Financial Institutions, Islamic Economics

1. INTRODUCTION: CONTRASTING SPIRITS

Weber (1930, p. 18) writes about the spirit of capitalism: Man is dominated by the making of money, by acquisition as the ultimate purpose of his life. Economic acquisition is no longer subordinated to man as the means for the satisfaction of his material needs . This stands in stark contrast to the clear Islamic prohibition on the pursuit of wealth for its own sake; for example:

(Q9:34) They who hoard up gold and silver and spend it not in the way of Allah, unto them give tidings (O Muhammad) of a painful doom.

In Islam, accumulation of wealth is permitted only for the purpose of spending in the ways prescribed by Allah. Pursuit of wealth for its own sake is not permitted. A more detailed discussion of this issue is given later in this paper.

1.1. The "Great Transformation" in the West

In the West also, in pre-capitalist era, the pursuit of wealth was not viewed favourably. According to the Bible, ove of money is the root of all evil. Ownership of wealth was a concession to human weakness, and Christian monks who took vows of poverty were honoured for this renunciation of the world. Dickens popular tale about Christmas shows the miser Scrooge is forced to repent, and learns that spending on others leads to happiness.

Polanyi (2001) has documented the great transformation that took place in Europe as a result of the transition to capitalist economic structures. An essential element of this transformation was a dramatic change in the attitudes towards the accumulation of wealth. his change is captured in haw s dictum that ack of money is the root of all evil. his came to be widely believed in the modern capitalist era: the accumulation of wealth will create a Heaven on Earth, and solve all problems of mankind. Zaman (2010) gives a brief summary of the relevant arguments and history.

1.2. The Functions of Banks

As a result of this transformation, financial institutions designed to support the acquisition, hoarding, preservation, and accumulation of wealth came into being for the first time. Central among these institutions is the Bank, which did not exist prior to the legitimisation of the pursuit of wealth. Among many others, Banks perform two key functions within a capitalist economy:

(1) By offering a small profit (interest), they encourage savings and accumulation.
(2) Furthermore, they collect savings from large numbers of small depositors, and transfer them to large investors, thereby causing an increase in concentration of wealth in the hands of the already wealthy.

Both of these functions are directly in conflict with Islamic teachings. Islam encourages spending on others:

2:274 Those who spend their possessions [for the sake of God] by night and by day, secretly and openly, shall have their reward with their Sustainer; and no fear need they have, and neither shall they grieve.

Islam also discourages miserliness and hoarding of wealth. In addition to Q9:34 cited earlier, note:

104:2 [Woe unto him] who amasses wealth and counts it a safeguard.

Also, Islam is strongly opposed to concentration of wealth in a few hands. It encourages spending by the wealthy on others in numerous verses. The Quran (59:7) states that acquired wealth should be given to kindred, wayfarers, orphans and the needy so that *"it may not (merely) make a circuit between the wealthy among you."* This has been universally interpreted as an encouragement for the circulation of wealth, and an admonishment against concentration of wealth in a few hands.

Thus both key functions of banks that we have identified are directly in conflict with Islamic teachings.

1.3. A Paradox of Islamisation

Many Muslim scholars have been convinced that Banks are necessary for the functioning of modern economic systems. On this basis, they have attempted to devise alternatives to Banks and Interest which would be compatible with Islamic laws. Some have simply declared that the Riba prohibited in the Quran is not the interest paid by modern banks. Others have devised more sophisticated equivalents of Riba, while trying to remain within the bounds of the hari ah. We argue that the answer to the question of whether Banks are necessary to modern economic systems is a paradoxical Yes and No.

Yes: Banks are Necessary within a Capitalist Economy. If we consider the capitalist economic system as a whole, banks perform key functions within this system. One of these functions is to channel funds from those who have to savings towards the capitalist/investors in the economy. Banks cannot function without interest which is used to attract these deposits. Theoretically it is possible to replace this fixed and secure interest with a variable rate based on Musharka contracts. Practically, the experiences of Islamic Banks show that small depositors cannot accept this uncertainty and risk. Therefore, instead of the preferred Islamic form of Musharkah, transactions essentially equivalent to riskless fixed interest contracts form the core of Islamic Banking today.

No, the Capitalist Economy itself is not Necessary: We cannot Islamise banks while functioning within a capitalist economy. However, there are many modes of economic organisation radically different from capitalistic ones. Banks will not be necessary IF we change the entire structure of the economy to an Islamic one. Some confusion on this issue has arisen due to a widespread conceptual misunderstanding among Islamic Economists. In the second quarter of the twentieth century, many Islamic countries gained independence and sought to implement a suitable economic system. At that time the key debate was between Capitalism and Communism. Islamic scholars compared the two and noted that free markets and private property were closer to Islamic concepts than government ownership of capital, and socialised production. While this is true on a broad level, closer examination reveals radical differences between Islamic and Capitalist ideas of free markets and private properties. From the times of the Prophet S.A.W. markets have been subject to regulations which are not present in capitalism. Also, private property is viewed as a trust and a responsibility, whereas capitalists consider property as an absolute right. Taking these differences into account creates great differences between capitalist and Islamic views on economics. Some of these contrasts are presented in Zaman (2013, Islam versus Economics).

One consequence of this analysis is that genuine Islamic institutions cannot be built as components of a capitalist economy. More radical reforms are required. In order to make this idea plausible, it is necessary to provide the sketch of a genuinely Islamic alternative to current financial institutional structures. At the present, this sketch may seem idealistic and impractical. It is important to note the current capitalist systems were similarly very remote and unrealistic when first conceived in the West. It was leadership, vision and power which led to the successful implementation of these ideas all over the world. Today, the Muslims need the courage to put forth and implement the bold alternative presented by Islam. Just as the leadership and vision of our prophet Mohammed S.A.W. changed the course of history, so the same opportunity awaits the Muslims today.

2. CONTRASTING VIEWS REGARDING HUMAN BEHAVIOUR

The key contrast between capitalism and Islam arises in response to the question what should we do with surplus (wealth in excess of our needs)? In capitalist societies, one is encouraged to save this wealth, and to use it to generate even more wealth. This is one of the primary functions of Banks, to encourage savings and accumulation. However, the Quran answers this precise question very differently:

> *(Q2:219) And they will ask thee as to what they should spend [in God's cause]. Say: "Whatever you can spare."*

Kahf (2003) cites several examples where the Prophet S.A.W. created (and also encouraged others to create) Awqaf—properties with revenues devoted to service of society. As we will demonstrate, corresponding to the spirit of generosity and spending on others, the central financial institution in an Islamic society is the Waqf—a trust or a foundation to provide social services to others. This difference in institutional structure arises from a fundamental difference in understanding the nature of human beings, and the objectives of social organisation.

2.1. Economic Models of Human Behaviour

The standard economic model of consumer behaviour portrays human beings as cold, callous and calculating. Consumers are cold—pure utility maximisers are not susceptible to emotional decision making and impulse purchases. They are callous— they will seek personal benefits even if it harms others, being indifferent to feelings of others. They are calculating—not just satisfied with making a profit, they calculate it to the last penny and seek to maximise it. Although it is understood that this is an idealisation and not an exact description, substantial efforts are made by economists to promote the idea that such assumptions are both empirically valid descriptions of human behaviour, and also that this behaviour is actually good for society.

Lack of Empirical Validity: Lionel Robbins (1935) asserted that the utility and profit maximisation assumptions of economic theory are simple and indisputable facts of experience. Current economic texts continue this tradition of claiming that the theory of firms and consumers is positive — it is an objective description of observed behaviour, rather than a normative description of what ideal rational behaviour might look like. In fact, there is massive evidence that assumptions of neoclassical utility theory are strongly in conflict with actual human behaviour; this evidence is summarised in a survey by Karacuka and Zaman (2012). Thus the economists model of human behaviour, widely taught in leading universities all over the world, is not empirically valid.

Lack of Normative Validity: The second widely claimed assertion of economic textbooks is that maximising agents within free markets create socially optimal outcomes. This is considered to be the message of the First Fundamental Welfare theorem of economic theory. For instance, a current leading economics textbook by Mankiw and Taylor (2007, pp. 7-9) asserts that:

Why do decentralised market economies work so well? Is it because people can be counted on to treat each other with love and kindness? Not at all. participants in a market economy are motivated by self-interest, and that the invisible hand of the market place guides this self-interest into promoting general economic well-being

This idea is also fundamentally wrong. Evidence of the failures of the invisible hand, and a guide to additional literature on the subject is summarised in Amir-ud-Din and Zaman (2013).

Despite the fact that both of these assumptions about human behaviour are wrong, capitalist institutions structures are built on the basis of these assumptions. At the level of individual, maximum freedom in all spheres (economic, political, social) is promoted as a key to fulfillment of worldly desires. At the group level, competition and survival of the fittest is promoted as the key to efficiency. This philosophy is best suited to a world of cold, callous and calculating individuals who have no concerns for an afterlife. Islam offers dramatically different conceptions of human behaviours and correspondingly different prescriptions for political, social and institutional structures.

2.2. Islamic Concepts About Human Behaviour

Islamic understanding of human behaviour is substantially more subtle and sophisticated than that of the Western economic models described earlier. The Quran explains that acquisitive and greedy tendencies are embedded within human beings:

> *Q3:14 ALLURING unto man is the enjoyment of worldly desires through women, and children, and heaped-up treasures of gold and silver, and horses of high mark, and cattle, and lands. All this may be enjoyed in the life of this world but the most beauteous of all goals is with God.*

The tendency towards evil has been made part of the human disposition. As the prophet Yusuf A.S. states in the Quran:

> *12:53 "Nor do I absolve my own self (of blame): the (human) soul is certainly prone to evil,*

It is this attraction of worldly goods and pleasures that are taken as fundamental within the Western canons of economic theory. It is assumed that the goal of economists is to help humans satisfy these desires.The principle of consumer sovereignty as expressed ina leading economics textbook by Samuelson and Nordhaus (1989, p. 26) states that economists must reckon with consumer wants and needs whether they are genuine or contrived .

However, the Quran states that men are not bound to obey these tendencies, and in fact, must struggle against and overcome them to succeed.

Allah aala has shown us the two highways of good and evil, and left us free to choose between them.

> *90:10 (We have) shown him the two highways (of good and evil)*
>
> *73:19 Lo! This is a Reminder. Let him who will, then, choose a way unto his Lord*

Those who surrender to their worldly desires choose the highway of evil, and will meet a bad fate. Those who overcome these worldly temptations and stay steadfast on the path to Allah will meet with a good fate.

> *79:37-41 For, unto him who rebelled; and preferred the life of this world; that blazing fire will truly be the goal! But unto him who shall have stood in fear of his Sustainer's Presence, and held back his inner self from base desires, paradise will truly be the goal!*
>
> *Q28:50 who could be more astray than he who follows [but] his own likes and dislikes without any guidance from God?*

Our life on the Earth is a test to see who chooses that pathway to his Lord, and who prefers the life of this world. Our goal as human beings is to choose the higher path, by fighting against the base desires, which have been implanted in our Nafs. This requires spiritual development, which can be achieved by various methods taught in Islam. The teachings of the Quran, personified by our Prophet S.A.W. are concerned with spreading the good, by teaching humans how to behave well. The Quran clearly sets out the functions of an Islamic state:

> *22:41 (Allah will help) those who, if we give them power in the land, establish regular prayer and give regular charity, enjoin the right and forbid wrong.*

Institutional structures of an Islamic society are designed to assist in this function, of making it easy for humans to choose the good pathways. Instead of promoting greed as a key to efficiency, Islamic societies must promote generosity and charity as part of their duties. There are several verses in the Quran condemning those who do not encourage the feeding of the poor —note the subtlety that it is not just the feeding of the poor, but rather the creation of a society in which all members are concerned about the feeding of the poor which is at issue. Thus in addition to generosity, Islamic societies must promote the spirit of cooperation. There are explicit Islamic teachings to create brotherhood, love among humans, cooperation, and a sense of responsibility for all members of society.

3. GENEROSITY AND WAQF

We can summarise the previous discussion by saying that capitalist societies promote fulfilment of individual desires within an institutional framework of competition. In contrast to greed and competition, institutional structures of an Islamic society promote generosity and cooperation. The number of Ayat in the Quran exhorting Muslims to be generous is greater than the number devoted to the four central pillars of salat, zakat, fasting and Hajj. As typical examples:

> *2:195 Spend your wealth for the cause of Allah, and be not cast by your own hands to ruin; and do good. Lo! Allah loveth the beneficent.*

Similarly, the Prophet Mohammad (peace be upon him) said, The generous man is near Allah, near Paradise, near men and far from Hell, but the miserly man is far from Allah, far from Paradise, far from men and near Hell. Indeed, an ignorant man who is generous is dearer to Allah than a worshipper who is miserly. [Tirmidhi]

In response to these commandments, Muslims have always been generous as a community. Even in present times, where Muslims as a whole are far from the practice of Islam, this continues to hold true. An ICM research Poll in 2012 found that Muslims were far ahead of all other communities in charitable giving. Similarly, a Pew Research Center Survey in 2012 documents that large percentages of Muslims make charitable donations. Najam (2007) provides similar data on the generosity of Muslims, relative to other communities. Income adjusted figures would provide even stronger evidence, since the Quran has praised those who give while being themselves in need.

3.1. Historical Role of Waqf in Islamic Societies

The spirit of generosity is embodied in the form of the institution of the Waqf, which has played a central role in Islamic history. The provision of health services, education, and other social welfare functions was efficiently handled by the Awqaf, so that nearly everyone in need had access to these services. The extensive network of the Awqaf and their functions is documented in Kahf (2003), who also provides references to the sources of this information:

Information extracted from the registers of Awqaf in Istanbul, Jerusalem, Cairo and other cities indicates that lands of Awqaf cover considerable proportion of total cultivated area. For instance, in the years 1812 and 1813 a survey of land in Egypt showed that Waqf represents 600,000 feddan (= 0.95 Acre) out of a total of 2.5 million feddan (Ramadan, p. 128); in Algeria the number of deeds of Awqaf of the grand mosque in the capital Algiers was 543 in the year 1841 (Ajfan, p. 326); in Turkey about one third of land was Awqaf (Armagan, p. 339); and finally in Palestine the number of Waqf deeds recorded up to middle of the sixteen century is 233 containing 890 properties in comparison with 92 deeds of private ownership containing 108 properties

Hoexter, *et al.* (2002) remarks on the extensive social services provided by these Awqaf in Islamic societies.

Prior to the twentieth century a broad spectrum of what we now designate as public or municipal services, e.g., welfare, education, religious services, construction and maintenance of the water system, hospitals, etc. were set up, financed and maintained almost exclusively by endowments, was documented in this stage. So was the fact that very large proportions of real estate in many towns and in the rural areas were actually endowed property.

Sait and Lim (2006) write that the system of *awqaf* succeeded for centuries in Islamic lands in redistributing wealth, leading to e uitable outcomes and the circulation of wealth in accordance with Quranic injunctions.

3.2. Necessity for Revival of Waqf

For complex historical reasons, this institution has become inefficient, ineffective and marginalised in modern Islamic societies. Sait and Lim (2005, p. write that he eclipse of the endowment *waqf*) has left a vacuum in the arena of public services, which the State has been unable to fill easily in many Muslim countries. The efforts to reconstruct Islamic societies must focus on re-vitalising the institution of Waqf, rather than on the Islamisation of western Banking. Many authors, including Kahf (2003) have noted the crucial role of Waqf in Islamic history, and have strongly recommended its revival as a key to the revival of an Islamic economy. Revival of the institution of Waqf depends on a key conceptual shift in understanding the role of the government.

The western form of Banking is not a *genuine* Islamic institution, in the sense that it is built to encourage and facilitate the spirit of hoarding, accumulation and concentration of wealth. Current efforts to Islamise banks by modifying the forms of banking transactions cannot affect the spirit of banking. This is why no institution analogous to the Banks have existed in the pre-colonial centuries of Islamic history. In contrast, the Waqf is a genuine Islamic institution, which embodies the Islamic spirit of generosity, and provision of service to the community for the sake of the love of Allah. These institutions performed a central role in provision of social services in pre-colonial times.

3.3. A Subtle but Radical Difference in Goals

A crucial difference between the Western approach to provision of social services and the Islamic one derives from the differing conceptions of human beings outlined earlier. Since Western economic theory assumes selfishness to be the basic characteristic of humans, the government must play a central role in the provision of social services. However, the Islamic government has the responsibility to promote and motivate excellence in human behaviour. Rather than just feeding the poor, it must urge the feeding of the poor. he fasts of Ramazan are designed to encourage empathy with the poor, and everyone is given the responsibility of taking care of the needy among his kin and among his neigbhors. While the Islamic government is the provider of the last resort, it is private organisations of the Awqaf which provided the vast majority of social services in the course of human history. Because these awqaf are run by local caretakers and take care of localised communities they have a wealth of local information which is essential to the efficient delivery of social services. Lacking this information, there is strong evidence that governments do not do well as direct providers of social service. The Islamic government must play an enabling role, encouraging and supporting local provision of social services; this will promote the feeling of responsibility, cooperation and community which is the goal of this method.

This fundamental issue needs to be highlighted because dominance of modern thinking has led to ignorance, even among Muslims. The goal of feeding of the poor is not directly poverty relief; this is a fringe benefit. Rather, the goal is the development of compassion, cooperation, and the attitude of obedience to the orders of Allah. That is why the dominant modern approach of Government provision of social service, which sacrifices the goal to obtain a fringe benefit, does not suit Islamic societies. A detailed discussion of this point is given in the Appendix of Zaman (2012, Lecture 1). Briefly, note that the Quran praises people who feed the poor *for the love of Allah*, and mentions that the purification of the heart is the objective of paying the poor due

> 92:18 he that spends his possessions [on others] so that he might grow in purity

Western economics regards humans as inherently self-centered and cannot conceive of the goal of changing humans to become generous, as an object of economic policy. Obviously, this goal cannot be achieved if the government takes up the responsibility of feeding the poor. Historically, Islamic governments did not view themselves as responsible for the provision of the social services; these were handled by individuals and an vast network of Awqaf. In this way, everyone in the society could expect to be fed, clothed, housed, and educated, since that was the collective responsibility of the society. Whereas banks are designed to bring depositors the earning of this world, *Waqf* are designed to generate earnings of the Akhirah. This difference in spirit is the essential difference between Islamic and Western worldviews. Just as banks compete to find the best investments in Dunya, so the *Awqaf* compete to find the best investments for the Akhira.

One of the key insights from Islamic history is that social services should be provided locally, by communities of generous individuals who are encouraged to care for others and take responsibility for the needy in their neighborhoods. Western models remove this responsibility from individuals and shift the burden for providing social service onto the government. This is highly in-efficient for many reasons.

4. TRUST AND DAR-UL-AMANAH

The prophet Mohammad S.A.W. was known as Al-Ameen (the trustworthy), and the quality of trustworthiness is one of the essential characteristics of Muslims. Allah commands us to fulfill our obligations:

5:1 O ye who believe! Fulfill your undertakings.

The practice of entrusting property to others for sakekeeping was common among the nomadic Arabs, and the Prophet himself, was the recipient of several such properties. This then is a genuine Islamic practice, where property and wealth is entrusted to others for safe-keeping. There is a large number of laws of the hari ah dealing with the concept of trust. e will only deal with some basic issues related to this concept.

Currently, there is a lot of effort to create Shariah compliant versions of financial instruments and transacting in use in Western Banking. If fact, efforts at Ijtihad are necessary in a different direction. We need to create modern forms of the ancient institution of Amanah. The dominant form of money today is paper currencies not backed by any real asset. This is a financial innovation of the twentieth century, which has never before existed in the history of mankind. Firstly we need an Islamic ruling on whether or not this is a legitimate financial instrument. This paper is concerned with providing an initial outline, a sketch of an Islamic financial system. Detailed discussion of the hari ah issues involved is not possible here. Three major issues need to be resolved, to implement the concept of safekeeping of deposits in modern times. Two of these are discussed below. The third deals with the idea of accumulating wealth over time by savings, and is dealt with in the next section.

4.1. Betrayal of Trust: Money and Banking

The institution of safekeeping of deposits is an old one. Roots of modern banking go back to the mid seventeenth century, when goldsmiths found it increasingly profitable to utilised gold deposited with them for lending, investments, and foreign exchange transactions. The idea of gambling with other people s money is thus built into the roots of modern banking. Several major banking crises over the past century have caused misery to millions. Muslims who think that establishing banks in Islamic countries is essential to economic success are simply ignorant of the history of banking, which we briefly review.

Banks gambled with the depositors and money and lost in a stock market crash that led to the Great Depression of 1929. Millions lost their life savings, jobs, and incomes as production plummeted. Strong banking regulations put into place prevented a repeat of the crisis until the 19 0 s, when eagan de-regulated the Savings and Loan Industry. The S&L industry lost no time in taking advantage of relaxations in laws to gamble on a large scale with the depositors money. The resulting banking crisis led to massive losses which wiped out the entire earning of the banking industry for the previous fifty years. This cycle was repeated when repeal of the Glass-Steagall act which prohibited banks from investing in stock markets eventually led to the global financial crisis of 2007-8. When we tabulate the costs and benefits, the costs of the banking crises far outweigh the gains from the banking system when considered over the course of the entire past hundred years. Thus, instead of rushing to blindly imitate western institutions, Muslims should examine the historical record of repeated disastrous failures of the Banking system.

The modern institution of unbacked paper currency is another case of violation of trust. Paper currency was initially fully backed by gold. Later on, it was realised that as long as people had confidence that there was gold to backup the currency, actual gold was not needed. his led to the concept of fractional reserve where only some fraction of the re uired backing in the form of gold was kept by the central banks. Later on, even this partial backing was withdrawn, and paper currency based purely on confidence, without any substantive real asset in the background. This confidence has been abused by nearly all governments by printing paper money without any backing. The evils and harms of this have been widely realised and proposals to go back to a 100 percent reserve have been floated by many, including an IMF team. Vadillo (2012) has strongly advocated the use of gold and silver, in the form of Dinars and Dirhams, as a solution to monetary problems being faced by Islamic countries.

4.2. Islamic Alternatives: Safekeeping of Real Assets

For those with money substantially in excess of their needs, the preferred mode is to spend it on others. This can be done in many different ways, but the Waqf is among the best ways. However, there are situations, discussed later in section 7, where accumulation of wealth is permissible within Islamic laws. This section deals primarily with people who have small amounts of money. Their primary need is for the safekeeping of this money, and this function was well known within Islamic societies. The Prophet S.A.W. himself kept assets in trust for many parties. et us use the name Dar-ul-Amanah to denote an institution which has the primary purpose of keeping assets of depositors safe. The replication of an institution for this purpose will required several innovations to suit the needs of modern times.

One of these problems is created by the fact that fiat currency is not a real asset, and is not suitable to store for deposit. This is because it has no real value, and the continuous printing of money by governments continuously erodes its value. So storing it will generally involve returning to the depositor less, in value terms, than what he put it in. Realistically, the small percentage offered on deposits basically only offsets the inflation, so existing banks only offer an illusion of increase to the small depositor. This is a commonly used justification for the provision of interest by Banks. While we do not agree with the provision of interest, we do agree that there is a problem that needs solution here.

A simple idea, based on Vadillo (2012) is to convert the deposits from currency to gold or silver at the moment the deposit is made. Then this real asset can be held for safekeeping, and returned to the depositor when he asks for it. This idea can be extended further, to additional real assets like land, or ownership of firms. There is some risk involved here, in that these assets can fluctuate in money terms. However, this risk is matched by the risk of inflation, since the value of the currency itself is not stable. There are various methods which can be used to create bundles of commodities which would be least susceptible to risk of variation, fulfilling the idea of maintaining value which is a requirement of Amanah.

4.3. Circulation of Wealth

Another problem with Amanah, if we think of it as simply storing real assets, is that it will block the circulation of money, which is vital to the economy and also commanded by Islam. The depositors are attracted to banks by a small interest payment. In turn, the pool of deposits is made available to investors by banks. If the assets are locked away in Darul Amanah, this will cause a serious decline in the amount of wealth in circulation in the economy.

A solution to this is suggested by the story of a companion of the Prophet S.A.W. who would not accept money as Amanah. He would instead accept it as a loan. Then he was free to spend this money on charitable projects. Repayment of loans is a requirement of Islamic law. This is so serious that the Prophet S.A.W. would inquire about loans of deceased people, and would refuse to offer the Salatul Janazah if there were unfulfilled loans. Thus the person offering a loan to the Dar-ul-Amanah should have confidence that he will be able to get it back. Islamic traditions also support the idea that the government can guarantee the repayment of these loans for additional safety.

Given that the Darul Amanah accepts deposits as loans from the depositors, how should it use these deposits? Conventional banks maximise worldly profits by investing in capital. In accordance with the spirit of Islam, Darul Amanah should use these funds to create human and social capital. There are many types of investments in human and social capital which provide good worldly returns. For instance, a vast amount of funding of higher education comes from donations by the alumni, which show that investment in education pays off in the long run. Also, recent studies show that the wealth of nations is more in the form of human capital rather than physical capital. Thus the investments in humans can actually produce more profits than the western financial systems which focus on physical investments.

4.4. Three Way Split

We propose, tentatively, that deposits at Darul Amanah may be split into three components. One portion could be a pure safekeeping, where the deposits will be physically stored and kept safe. A second portion could be designated for investment purposes. These deposits could earn money, but would be at risk for loss as well. How the Darul Amanah would handle these funds is discussed in the section 7 below. The third portion could be designated as a loan for social purposes—Qarz-e-Hasna—from the depositor to the Darul Amanah. It is possible to design institutional structures to guarantee these loans, so that the depositor need not fear that the loan may not be returned. This portion would be spent on projects which would develop human and social capital, but may have uncertain payoffs. If the portfolio of these projects is managed well, there would be adequate returns for sustainability, but the goal would be to maximise the profits of the Akhirah with this portion of the deposits. There are many Ahadeeth that suggest that if we try to earn the Akhirah, then Allah aala will also provide with the blessings of this world. It seems likely that if we try to promote social welfare, we will create many positive externalities which will create strong positive real returns as well.

5. QARZ-E-HASNA: THE KEY TO SOCIAL CAPITAL

In genuine Islamic societies, there is a substantial amount of private spending on social welfare. There are two instruments which are crucial in achieving this goal. The first is donations, which are just given away without any (worldly) quid-pro-quo. Both Quran and Hadeeth is full of encouragement for making such donations. The second method is Qarz-e-Hasna, which is spending in the path of Allah without *expectation* of returns in this world. If the party to which the loan is given is eventually able to re-pay, then we may get the loan back, but otherwise not. Allah aala encourages the giving of such loans as follows:

> 2:245 Who is he that will loan to Allah, a beautiful loan, (QARZE-E-HASNA) which Allah will double and multiply many times? It is Allah that gives (you) want or plenty and to Him shall be your return

Western theories of human behaviour assume that selfishness is the base of human behaviour, and charitable impulses are occasional deviations which cannot be sustained in the long run. Therefore, conventional theories of microfinance focus heavily on the idea that loans to the poor must be not only be repaid by the poor but the lender should actually make some profits—if this is not done, then the mechanism is not considered sustainable. Under the influence of these western ideas, some Muslims have also stated that the idea of expecting cooperation and generosity is idealistic and impractical. If this is so, then the Quran is also being unrealistic and impractical in exhorting Muslims to develop these qualities.

In fact, history testifies to the change brought about in the Arabs by the message of Islam, which led them from being backwards nomads to leaders of the world. Allah aala Q :10 mentions His favour on the Arabs that you were enemies, He joined your hearts in love, so that by His Grace, ye became brethren . Thus changing behaviours from competitive to cooperative is not only possible, but Islamic teachings provide us with the methodology to achieve such change. Furthermore, this methodology was demonstrated in practice by the Prophet S.A.W.

Investing in social and human capital creates very strong positive externalities. Perhaps this is what is referred to in the following Ayah:

> *2:268 Satan threatens you with the prospect of poverty and bids you to be niggardly, whereas God promises you His forgiveness and bounty; and God is infinite, all-knowing*

If we spend on other, especially via Qarz-e-Hasna, we take a risk that we may need the money in the future, but it will not be available to us. However in a society where the cultural norm is to spend on others in need, we can expect to be helped by others. This means that the need for precautionary savings is substantially reduced. he fear of poverty will not materialise if the spirit of cooperation is created. It will also create trust, which has been recognised to be crucial factor in promoting economic growth recently. In fact, it is creation of this feeling of cooperation and community which is directly the goal of Islamic teachings. Spending on others is a means of achieving this goal:

> *3:92 [O believers] never shall you attain to true piety unless you spend on others out of what you cherish yourselves;*

This reverses secular teachings according to which provision of social services is a goal, and charity is a means of achieving this goal.

6. ACCUMULATION OF WEALTH

There are many legitimate ways to spend in the path of Allah. Taking care of oneself and ones family and close relations is part of Islamic obligations, and someone who seeks to increase his wealth in order to fulfill these duties is acting according to the rules of hari ah. It is only the irrational pursuit of wealth for its own sake —which is the spirit of capitalism—that is prohibited in Islamic law. One extremely important restriction here is that earnings must be Halal—permissible in Islamic law. This means that some service must be provided to acquire earning. In Islam, unlike capitalism, mere ownership of wealth is not considered as a service to society. Thus, the possession of wealth does not entitle one to earn money; this is the justification for the prohibition on interest. Those who are wealthy, and want to earn money on this wealth, must participate in the risks of doing business for the acquisition of wealth. Modern investment banks actually provide this service—they allow investors to participate in risks and profits of doing business. Versions of this type of banking would be permissible in Islamic law, and could be among the genuine Islamic financial institution necessary to replace banks. For example, our Prophet S.A.W. participated in, and led, caravans financed on this basis. Also, since accumulation of wealth must be directed towards some hari a permissible purpose, special institutions for savings would provide more efficient vehicles for customers saving for some common purpose. Bare outlines of these ideas are presented below.

6.1. General Principles for Accumulation of Wealth

Islamic teachings on wealth are subtle and sophisticated, showing that wealth can be a curse and also a blessing. Because of this dual nature of wealth, many writers have gone astray by over-emphasising one side or the other. To begin with, this our worldly possessions are a test:

> *8:28 and know that your worldly goods and your children are but a trial and a temptation, and that with God there is a tremendous reward.*

If we earn money in a Halal way, save and accumulate it for Halal purposes, and spend it in Halal ways, without developing the disease of the love of money in our hearts, then this wealth is a blessing. For those who fail in this trial, like Qaroon, the wealth is a curse. This dual nature of wealth is clearly pointed out in a Hadeeth cited in section 9, chapter 9 of Hikayut-us-Sahabah, Fazail-e-Amal:

> **Hakim! Wealth has a deceptive appearance. It appears to be very sweet (but it is really not so). It is a blessing when earned with contentment of heart, but there is no satisfaction in it when it is got with greed.**

To earn the money in a halal way is an essential requirement of Islam. A Muslim who has absorbed these teachings would not participate in the numerous get-rich-quick schemes which are widely advertised. This is because legitimate earnings must be compensation for some service provided, and earning something for nothing is permissible and Halal only under very restricted circumstances.

Similarly, being self-sufficient, and providing support to ones dependents is an Islamic obligation. Earning and accumulating wealth for this purpose is considered as worship. Those who happen to become needy are encourage to hide their needs, and not beg from others. At the same time, those with excess wealth are encouraged to seek out the needy, recognising them by signs (since they will not be asking) and provide for them in an honorable way.

If these Islamic norms prevail in a society, the need for accumulation of wealth by individuals will be substantially reduced, for three reasons:

(1) The norms of helping each other in times of need will reduce the need for precautionary savings. It has been noted by Anthropologists that no one goes hungry in subsistence economies because of strong norms of sharing.
(2) Islam strongly encourages simple lifestyles. Sustaining these will require substantially less wealth than the luxurious lifestyles that are promoted as ideals in capitalist economies.
(3) Islamic teaching prohibit Israf and Tabzeer, or wasteful consumption. Less money will be needed, and more will be available to spend on others.

The net effect of this would be that there would much more spending on human and social capital, and much less on capital—machines and factories—in an Islamic society. Interestingly, a lot of recent research shows that these invisibles (human capital and trust) are much stronger determinants of economic growth than conventional physical capital. In capitalist societies, a large proportion of wealth is spent on making profits for a very small proportion of the population, while a small proportion is spend on providing social services. Islamic societies would reverse these priorities.

6.2. General Purpose Institutions

These would be institutions which allow people with excess wealth to participate in trading or investment. These differ from conventional banks in some crucial respects. Profits earned by participants are compensation for risks of business, which is legitimate in Islam. A service is provided to society by funding a risky business venture. In contrast, conventional business allows for increases in wealth without any service being provided. So-called Islamic banks attempt to replicate this western model, by allowing people with wealth to earn money without taking any risks or providing any service to society. This creates the same ill effect of concentration of wealth which are produced by conventional banks. Nienhaus (2012) has discussed the deviation between the claims and the reality of Islamic banks.

Some relevant considerations are listed below:

(1) We do not expect small depositors to put money into investment bank. These clients will be catered to by the Dar-ul-Amana. Only relatively wealthy clients would seek to increase their wealth. However, if clients designate some portion of their small deposits for investments, the Dar-ul-Amana could aggregate such deposits and select relatively low risk investments on their behalf.
(2) Those with wealth in excess of their needs would be eligible to use investment banks, but should be offered Shariah consultative services. The preferred use for excess wealth is to spend it on others.

Shaitan scares people into excess savings and away from generosity by raising the fear of poverty in their hearts. Shariah consultants should be able to offer advice on how to differentiate between realistic and legitimate requirements of financial security, and excessive and exaggerated demands for the accumulation of wealth.

(3) The purpose for seeking an increase in excess wealth should be clarified, since it is not permissible to accumulate wealth without a specific, legitimate purpose. Also, it is an Islamic teaching to actually encourage those with excess wealth to spend it on the needy—note the condemnation of those who did not urge the feeding of the poor. Thus, the Shariah advisor should encourage those with excess wealth to create Waqf, or otherwise serve the poor with this excess wealth.

6.3. Special Purpose Savings Institutions

As discussed earlier, unlike capitalism, Islam does not allow unconstrained pursuit of wealth. There are some special purposes for which savings is permissible or even recommended. Many benefits can be derived by the creation of special purpose savings organisations which target specific needs of Muslims. A key to this discussion is the idea that these organisations will provide real services, not just financial ones. This is because earnings must be tied to provision of services to be Halal. In this context, specialised organisations are much more capable of efficient provision of services targeted to clientele saving for a specific purpose.

For example, it is permissible and desirable to save money for performing Hajj. An extremely successful financial organisation which caters to people saving for this purpose is Tabung Haji in Malaysia. There are many benefits available from specialisation. If a large organisation has collected funds for the purpose of Hajj, it can target its investments in transportation services, residences in Mecca and Medina, and other areas to facilitate its customers. It can gather and distribute specialised knowledge of relevance to the target audience. The success of Tabung Haji suggests that similar savings institutions, which obviously have no parallels in the west, can also be successful in other Islamic countries.

A second area for which savings is permissible is to purchase a house. The Quran (16:80) mentions houses and tents as gifts of Allah to humankind. According Hadeeth in Musnad Ahmad (1368), a house is one of the three determinants of happiness of the son of Adam. Models for specialised savings institutions designed to help customers to build or purchase homes exist in the form of Building Societies. These would have to adapted to serve Islamic needs. In accordance with the vision of providing a wide range of services, Islamic Building societies could own apartment complexes which would provide temporary housing to investors in process of acquiring their own houses. It could provide a range of services like evaluation of properties and land, as well as provision of expert builders, contractors, architects etc.

A third area for which people save is health emergencies. A cooperative health model where people pool resources to purchase common health services would be an Islamic alternative to the insurance concept, which is adversarial in nature. Such institutions—cooperatives for health care—already exist in the west, and could be adapted to serve Islamic purposes. Similarly, auto clubs provide a wide range of services for owners of automobiles. Such institutions could also provide the service of allowing customers to save up to buy a car, thereby creating a special purpose savings fund for car purchases.

The distinguishing feature of Islamic institutions is that earnings are based on the provision of real services. This involves having a broader vision than the narrow restriction to purely financial services, as currently popular in the west. The concept of making profits by any means, without considering whether or not a service of some value has been provided, leads to substantial social harm. There is a large amount of materials documenting the greed on Wall Street and the harm it has led to. For instance, Greg Smith (March 2011) recently resigned from Goldman-Sachs after accusing the firm of making profits by misleading and deceiving customers regarding investments.

7. CONCLUDING REMARKS

In this paper we have outlined a structure of financial institutions which would conform to the Islamic spirit of generosity, cooperation, and provision of service. As we have seen, these institutions differ substantially from capitalist counterparts, which are based on the spirit of hoarding and accumulation of wealth.

There are four or more functions provided by modern banks. Genuine Islamic alternatives provide different and separate institutions for each function. For the small depositor who want to keep his money safe, we need to construct Dar-ul-Amanah. A proper emulation of the concept of keeping wealth safe requires some innovation in the modern world where most wealth is in the form of unbacked paper currency. For those with wealth in excess of their needs, spending it on others is the preferred use. However, this excess wealth can also be saved if the accumulation is to be used for spending in the way of Allah. Several institutions adapted to special purposes which are permissible in the Shariah have been discussed. A differentiated structure of institutions is needed because each institution should provide real services to its clients, in order to justify earning profits. The purely financial services can be handled by a single institution, as in the western model. However, numerous crises have shown the spectacular failures of this model, which has inflicted heavy costs on society as a whole.

As important as the form is the spirit behind the form. The Islamic institutions are designed to generate cooperation, community and trust. Islamic teachings do not display duality that is, the form is not separate from the spirit. It is not that we must first pay attention to spiritual development, and then later create Islamic institutions. Rather, the two efforts go hand in hand. The existence of Awqaf will create opportunities to spend on others, which will create generosity. The spirit of generosity will facilitate the creation of Awqaf. Similarly in other dimensions, the form and spirit go together.

The teachings of Islam created a revolution in the world some fourteen centuries ago. Today the world is again enveloped in the darkness of Jahilliya, and these teachings have the same potential to enlighten the world. This is the challenge facing us as Muslims today.

REFERENCES

Amir-ud-Din, Rafi and Asad Zaman (2013) Failures of the Invisible Hand. (Draft).

Hoexter, Miriam, Schmuel N. Eusenstadt, and Nehemia Leutzion (2002) *The Public Sphere in Muslim Societies.* New York: State University of New York.

Kahf, Monzer (2003) The Role of Waqf in Improving the Ummah Welfare. Presentation at the International eminar on a f as a Private egal Body organised by the Islamic University of North Sumatra, Medan, Indonesia January 6-7.

Karacuka, M. and A. Zaman (2012) The Empirical Evidence Against Neoclassical Utility Theory: A Review of the Literature. *International Journal for Pluralism in Economics Education* 3:4, 366 414.

Mankiw, N. G. and M. P. Taylor (2007) *Macroeconomics European Edition (PV) 6th edition.* Worth Publishers.

Najam, Adil (2007) *Portrait of a Giving Community: Philanthropy by the Pakistani—American Diaspora.* Harvard: Harvard University Press.

Nienhaus, olker 2011 Islamic inance Ethics and hari ah aw in the Aftermath of the risis: oncept and Practice of hari ah ompliant Finance. *Ethical Perspectives—Katholieke Universiteit Leuven* 18.4, 591 623.

Polanyi, K. (2001) *The Great Transformation: The Political and Economic Origins of Our Times.* Beacon Press.

Robbins, Lionel (1935) *An Essay on the Nature and Significance of Economic Science.* (2nd Edition). London: Macmillan and Co.

Sait, Siraj and Hilary Lim (2005) *Islamic Land and Property Research Series.* Nairobi: UN-Habitat. Series of Eight Position Papers. 1. Islamic and theories and Applications . 2. Islamic and enure and eforms. . Islamic aw, and and Methodologies. 4. Islamic Human ights and

and. 5. Muslim omen s ight to Property. 6. Islamic Inheritance aws and ystems. . Islamic Endowments (Waqf) and Indigenous Philanthropy, 8. Islamic redit and Microfinance .

Sait, Siraj and Hilary Lim (2006) *Land, Law and Islam: Property and Human Rights in the Muslim World.* London: Zed Books.

Samuelson, Paul A. and William Nordhaus (1989) *Economics.* (13th Edition). McGraw Hill Publishers.

Vadillo, Umar (2012) Towards Just Monetary System: Introducing Dirham and Dinar Currency. Lecture sponsored by IRI & IIIE at International Islamic University, Islamabad.

Weber, Max (1930) *The Protestant Ethic and the Spirit of Capitalism.* Transl. Parsons, Talcott, London: Allen and Unwin.

Zaman, Asad (2010) The Rise and Fall of Market Economies. *Review of Islamic Economics* 14: 2. Reprinted in Chapter 2 of *Civilisation and Values: Open Civilisation— Istanbul Approach.* Eds: M al inta , I urulay, and . ent rk, Istanbul: I O , pp. 140 178.

Zaman, Asad (2012) *Principles of an Islamic Education.* Lecture 1 of Lectures on Islamic Economics. (Draft), available from: https://sites.google.com/site/zamanislamicecon/lectures

Zaman, Asad (2013) Islam versus Economics. Chapter 3 in *Oxford University Handbook on Islam and the Economy.* Ed: Kabir Hassan and Mervyn Lewis. Oxford University Press. (Forthcoming).

www.ingramcontent.com/pod-product-compliance
Lightning Source LLC
Chambersburg PA
CBHW070736180526
45167CB00004B/1775